ASIA'LYNN HARRIS

The Power of a Teen Entrepreneur

Passion + Purpose = CEO

Copyright © 2022 by Asia'Lynn N Harris

All rights reserved.

This book or any portion thereof may not be reproduced or used in any manner whatsoever without the express written permission of the publisher except for the use of brief quotations in a book review

Printed in the United States of America

First Printing, 2022

ISBN: 978-1-7347985-5-5

Sophisticated Real-Life Publications

P.O. Box 988

Abbeville, La 70511

www.acolefit.com

Table of Contents

Book Description viii

Introduction 1

Growing Up 3

My Mom Is My Hero 9

Cheerleading 14

Pageants 20

Discovering Your Passion And Talents 24

Do You Have What It Takes To Be A Teen Entrepreneur? 43

Building My Business And Branding Process 128

Welcome to the World of Entrepreneurship

BOOK DESCRIPTION

Are you a teenager filled with passion? Do you have a business idea in mind? As teenagers, we have many dreams and plans for the future, but the mistake most of us make is believing that we will always have the time to start working toward our end later. Yeah! I understand there is no need to put pressure on yourself; we don't have bills to pay, and we want to enjoy our teenage years and focus on the future when the time is right. However, if you could check the statistics of young entrepreneurs worldwide, that should be a good motivator.

In this book, I will be sharing my entrepreneurial journey, motivation, success, interests, passions, and accomplishments thus far. I will be taking you through how I was able to combine schooling, cheerleading, pageantry, and, of course, running my clothing line. We all have potential and don't have to wait before pursuing our dreams.

This book was specifically written for every young mind out there and every young person who has a business idea in them. You could turn it around and make the most out of it if you have a hobby. Most importantly, this is an immediate wake-up call for children, teenagers, and young minds. The time is now!

INTRODUCTION

We are approaching a time when people are quitting their 9-5 jobs and are exploring becoming their own CEO. The game is changing, and I believe every young person should consider this opportunity. I am not insinuating everyone should give up on corporate life. Still, I am talking about how we can explore the possibilities of multiple income streams even at a young age. Every teen should already seek to become self-sufficient by becoming a business owner.

Everyone has a passion or talent that will add value to others. It would help if you explored how you can turn your passion and skills into something valuable that will give you a sustainable life now and in the future. Now is the time to see yourself not just as a young person, but as a unique individual with so much to work toward achieving success. You don't have to follow the norms but your unique talents by learning practical business skills to prepare yourself for financial success.

You need to start at a young age because exploring new concepts and information is more straightforward before life patterns become established. Do you desire to learn a skill, such as dance, soccer, cheerleading, basketball, or painting to name a few? This is the time to get your mind on board and put in your best. Give it a trial, it won't hurt! Why not put in your best now and gain financial skills that will ensure financial security and stability later in the future?

The goal is to identify your skills, interests, and conduct as early as possible, as these are usually indicators of your talents. You can find a mentor to guide you in learning how to discover your gifts and assist you in matching your skills to commercial prospects. By doing so, you are putting yourself on the path to a successful future. The idea is to have deep thoughts and list your personal qualities, interests, and passions. Your hobbies and interests are usually indicators of something you can excel at, which is an excellent reason to pay attention to them. It is easy to accomplish anything once we set our minds to it.

Take note of everything. You might have many interests, which may confuse you straightforward about which one you can excel at. Think about your innate personality and the ones you engage with the most. Then concentrate on turning these abilities into a profitable business that will give you the confidence you need to succeed.

GROWING UP

As a young girl, my mom always took pictures of me. I would have professional pictures taken at least once a month. My mom told me that when she was pregnant with me and had an ultrasound, the sonographer said to her, "Look at how she's posing. It would be best to get ready because she will be so amazing. She will be full of greatness." My mom didn't realize the sonographer was speaking greatness over my life and that it would come to pass. At one point in my life, we lived in what was known as the "housing authority." Life was adventurous and bold. The buildings were built of brown bricks and we had some young and elderly neighbors. We were living in a two-bedroom apartment. As a toddler, my room was decorated with everything from Dora the Explorer. I had my curtains, comforter set, lamp, TV, and even a kitchen set of Dora in my room. I watched her episodes every day. I was always out, discovering new things, playing with friends, or driving around in the little car my grandpa had bought me.

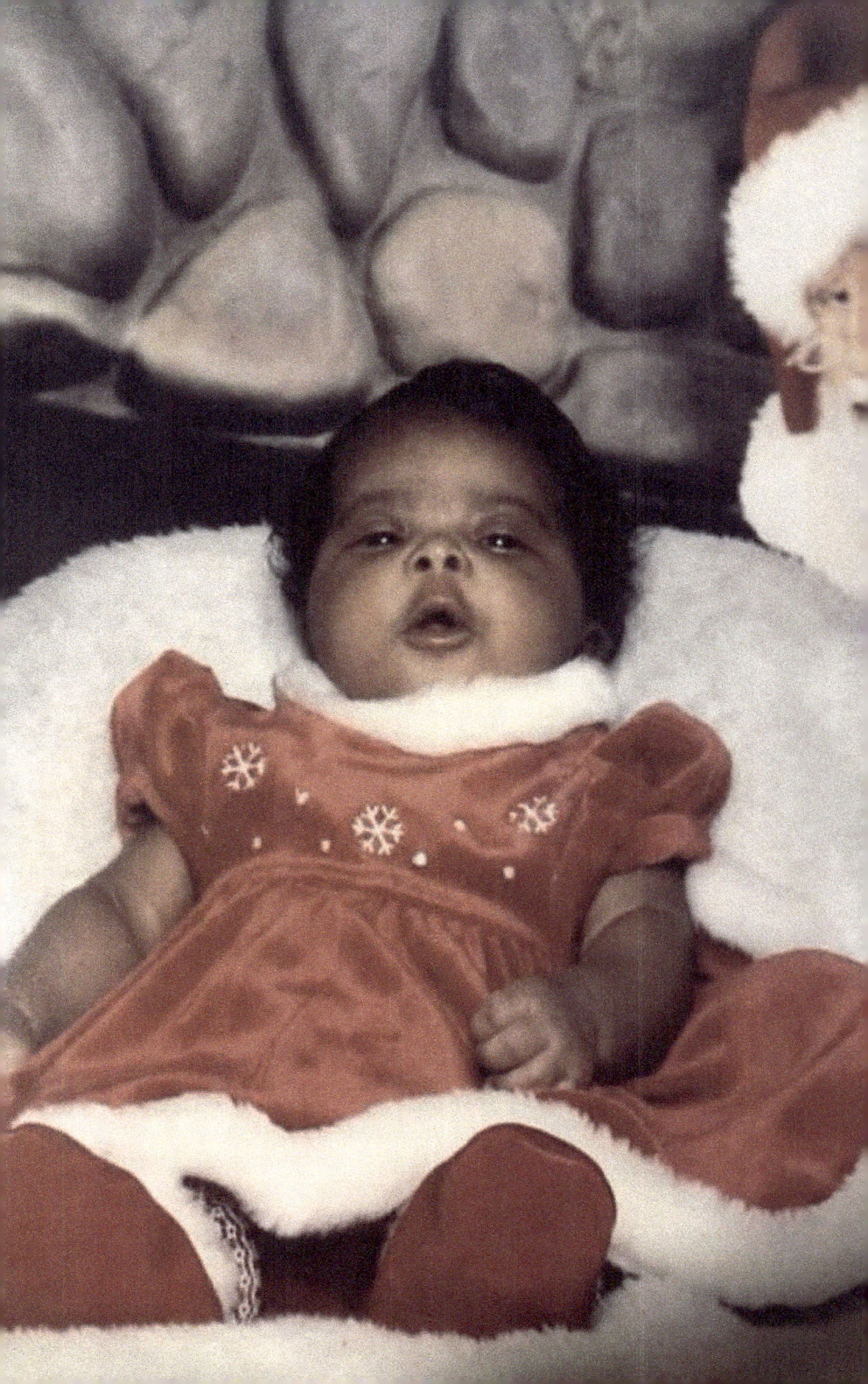

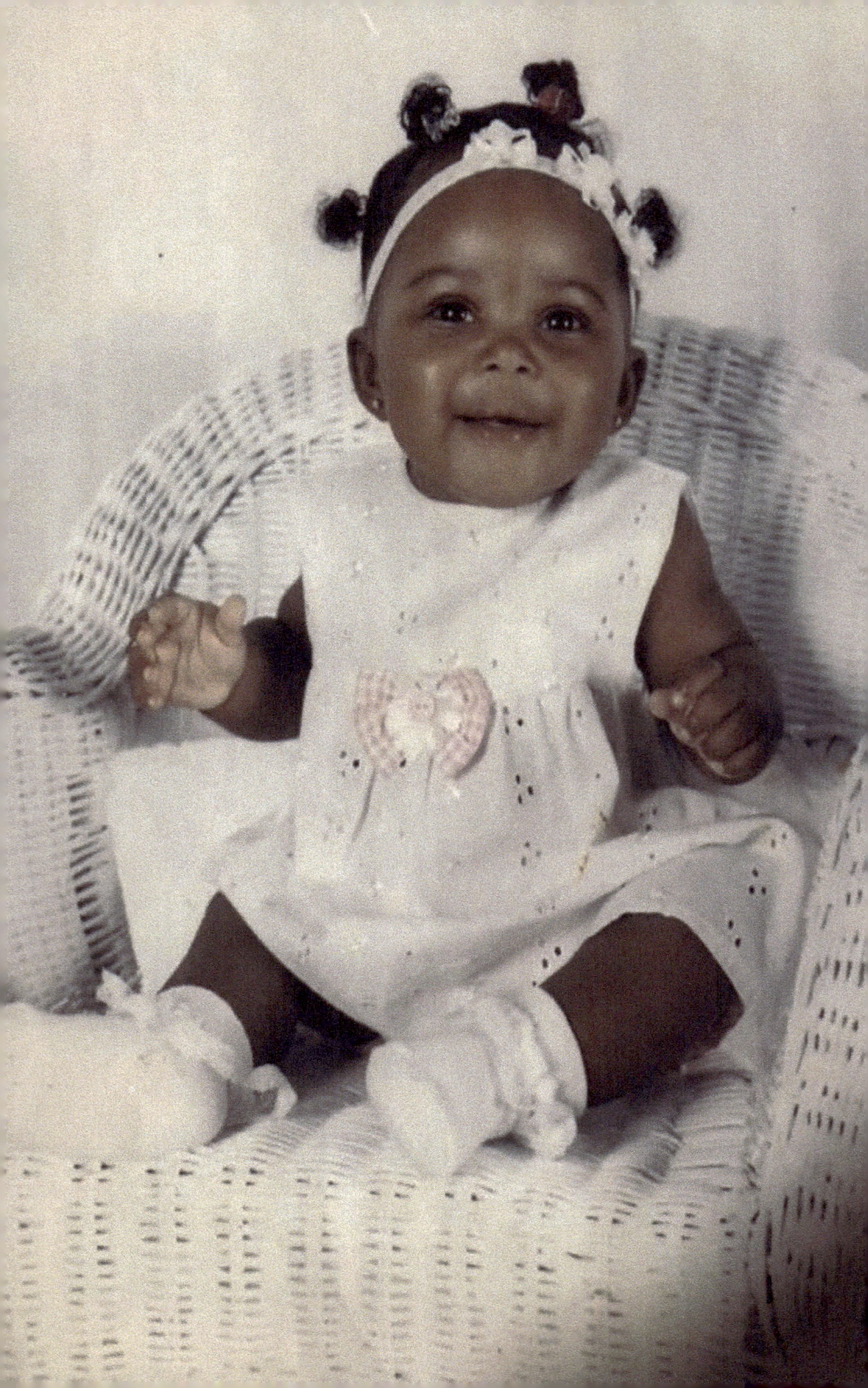

Aside from me having my fun time, I was also a busy girl involved in many activities. I was into dancing, including tap, hip hop, jazz, and ballet. I started playing the piano at the age of four. My mom enrolled me in piano lessons. And, of course, I participated in pageants. I was crowned Miss Abbeville at a local pageant in my town. I was also an honor roll and principal's list student who loved to be the life of the party in school! Life was exciting when I was young because I constantly switched between dance recitals, piano recitals, and pageants. Of course, when you are a young child, life is easy because you never see the struggles that lie hidden from you. As I got older, I understood that my mom raised me independently. Often, times got hard financially, which held my mother and me back from being able to chase our dreams. There were many years when I was in and out of dancing and piano because my mom couldn't afford both. I grew up watching my mother do her best to make ends meet when it came to taking care of me. Right before I began middle school, a lady who took notice of my talents explained to my mom about an art school I should attend in a town near us. However, I had to audition to be able to be accepted into the school. If I were accepted into the school, we would have to move to that town to attend the school.

I remember my mom taking me to the audition. I felt like I was on the TV show American Idol, where we would perform with our very own number in our hands and then be released back to our parents to wait for feedback on whether we would be accepted. Two weeks later, we received a letter in the mail that I was accepted into the School of Arts. So, we moved to a city twenty minutes away from our hometown so that I could participate in the L.J. Alleman Arts Academy. I auditioned to be in this school by playing the piano and got in! I continued going there throughout sixth and seventh grade until we moved back home due to the lack of funding. It is difficult to say this was the norm for my mom and me, but it was. But generally, no matter how many setbacks we had, we still completed many accomplishments.

MY MOM IS MY HERO

My biggest supporter who happens to be my mom, has been the drive behind everything I've accomplished. My mom is a single mother who has managed to earn her MBA in business and owns her own publishing company. She is also an author and an entrepreneur. I received the passion for entrepreneurship from my mom as I watched her do it consistently on her own. Making things happen for me was not easy, but it was always done. I have learned from my mother that you must work hard for everything you want to achieve in life, and it may be difficult at times, but you will be proud of yourself in the end. I have also had the opportunity to realize that not everyone will jump right in to support you and that sometimes, you do have to cut certain people out of your life to continue on your path to success. My mom and I have traveled to many places, and whether it was to sell my clothing line or compete in a pageant, we made the best of it, even if we were let down at times. As a young entrepreneur, I am still learning how to grow my business and luckily for me, I have my mom and her smarts to help me thrive until it is my turn to earn the ambitious degrees in business.

CHEERLEADING

Although I am a full-time CEO and a high-school student, I also share a passion for cheerleading. I receive many questions about how I manage it all, but the only true answer is to be fully consumed by whatever drives you! I discovered my love for cheerleading as an upcoming freshman in high school and have continued with it ever since. The realization of growth is strong when it comes to meeting other young girls and learning the ways of leadership together. Cheerleading can sometimes be complex, but I have always kept my smile and confidence when performing!

    I started to find my love for cheerleading in middle school, although I did cheer for the little league when I was seven years old for a short while. I knew that when trying out for the cheer team in middle school, I needed to have some experience, being that I hadn't participate in cheer for a while, so I joined tumbling. Because I am short, I had to go through extra steps to stretch out my body when I started tumbling. Before I could become well enough in tumbling to try out for the cheer team, I was taken out due to financial reasons. My mom tried her best but struggled to care for me and afford extra-curricular activities. When cheer tryouts came, I kept my head up and tried out, but sadly, I did not make the team. The other girls were super trained.

After moving back to my hometown for high school, I decided to give cheer another go with training from one of the former cheerleaders. I made the team and fell in love with cheer. My early years were great because we had experienced cheerleaders who kept all the traditions alive. Meeting other cheer teams and learning new things from them was super fun. They were kind and taught us well, but when they left, and it was time for my year group to take charge, things were not the same anymore. But keeping those memories of the great times we had will forever be the best thing about cheerleading. We took pictures of us traveling and cheering for our team at games on Friday nights. I also went to cheer camp in Florida and received an award for All American Cheer. I was super excited and proud of myself because I had worked hard, and it had paid off.

PAGEANTS

I began to steal the spotlight just as a baby when I began my first hobby of pageants. This is where I first discovered my confidence while growing up. I was always the little girl who befriended competitors and shared kindness with all. I was also so outgoing that even as a toddler, I refused to let my mother walk me on stage; I wanted to do it all alone! I have won many pageants while competing, but also lost some. Many times, it was just my mom traveling to pageants with me, but when I stepped on the stage, the whole crowd would cheer for me. You would think that they were my family as well. Pageants, to me, were never about the looks or the crown. It was mainly about me being able to show the judge and audience my confidence and inspire other girls. When being in pageants, you meet many different people, I met lots of different girls, but the ones who stood out to me were the shy ones. This is because I immediately went up to them and asked to be their friend because although on stage, I am the brightest factor in life, off stage, I am also very quiet, and I know what it feels like to be not so confident.

Aside from all the positive outlooks, there were also many negative times. My mother was a single mom with very little support, so sometimes, it was difficult for us to continue doing pageants. As a child, you don't understand why you are participating in something for a while and then suddenly removed from it. This situation came down to my participation in some pageant categories or none because my mom could not afford it. From this, I grew and became a stringer along the journey of having a single parent, and I still have a whole new outlook on life today. Even though we went through many trying times, I always ensured my best when stepping out on stage, win or lose.

DISCOVERING YOUR PASSION AND TALENTS

The best way to take charge of the world is to identify your talents. Find a way to enhance your career and discover new possibilities around you. If you have already discovered your abilities, you don't have to wait for the golden opportunity, but instead, find a way to make the best out of it. This chapter is for you if you haven't yet discovered your talents. When you discover your talents, you have the potential for greater productivity and fulfillment. Every successful and high-performing person in organizations or entrepreneurship today mainly started with their talents and passions. You can easily make something out of your talent when you can figure it out.

Your talent is more than your skills and passion; it defines you! The exciting demonstration of your unique skills will benefit you and the world. Your passion and talents come from within. It is what you are passionate about. However, I would like for you to take your time. Don't rush so you don't make mistakes.

Common mistakes

There are a lot of common mistakes young people make when trying to discover their talents. Here is a list of possible errors you should avoid:

No rushing

Maybe you just read a book about a young entrepreneur and feel that is it! I must start now, and you begin to sign up for different activities without considering what you truly and deeply enjoy doing. It will be challenging to run so many activities simultaneously, and this can pressure you because of competitions, deadlines, and more. This wears you out physically, and worse, it could also affect your grades. You don't want that! You can simply list all you feel you are interested in and go for the top three you are convinced within yourself you can effectively balance with other activities. You will achieve better results when you focus on one, two, or three skills. You'll be more focused on making the best of your skills, and your schedule will be more relaxed. You don't have to rush into discovering your passions and skills; instead, take your time to avoid making mistakes.

Comparison

People often compare themselves to others. You should avoid this at all costs. Everyone has unique abilities. Just because your friend is taking a dance lesson it doesn't mean you should also take a dance class. The key here is to let passion lead you. When your passion leads you, there's an excellent chance of challenges you may come across, but don't quickly give up. Don't compare yourself to anyone else; your passion is from the heart. It is possible to share a similar passion with a friend, no dispute! My focus here is to make sure it is what you want and that you are not influenced by comparison to others.

Parent/guardian

Sometimes, parents like to define skills for their children. They were excellent and successful in a particular field, so they feel that should be your passion, too. If you don't have a passion for it and don't even enjoy doing it, have a deep talk with your parent or guardian and let them know the skills you are genuinely passionate about. You don't have to go with the flow because that's what your parents want. I am sure your parents will be proud of you when they see that you have your passions, skills, and talents. Explain to them that you can only excel at what you are genuinely passionate about and that they should support you.

How to discover your passion and skills

Make a list of the activities that you find rewarding and significant.

Take time to brainstorm about all the regular activities you already participate in and write them down. This can include all the activities you are already a part of in school, work duties, hobbies, and anything else that makes you feel special and truly happy. Take note of the activities in which you often lose track of time. Also, consider your future ambitions: everything you have always wished to become. Think of the jobs you know that will fulfill you in the future and those you have never considered yourself doing. This can also help you identify the skills you are genuinely passionate about.

Consider your talents

You can have a skill you are naturally good at, or a skill set you have developed. This is an indication that you are passionate about it. Consider your natural talent. It may be playing guitar, singing, photography, and so on, or a skill you have made yourself available to learn strictly because you enjoy doing it. If you can't pick out these skills, pay close attention to the stuff you do effortlessly, which you get many compliments on. You might not pay attention to this stuff because it comes to you naturally, but by paying close attention to compliments from others, you will be able to recognize your true talents. You might think, *I play the guitar, but so does Mary,* and not give it any special attachment. However, people who see you play can recognize talent when they see it; they can see your uniqueness and the passion and effort you put into it while playing. You don't have to be the best at something you do before you recognize your talent; all you need is to discover it and, with effort and hard work, make the best out of it.

Also, remember that you don't have to be good at something to be passionate about it. So long as you enjoy engaging in the activity, you can still become passionate about it. Don't ever undermine yourself and limit what you can achieve with your success.

Still can't figure it out?

If you are confused and you can't get yourself to pinpoint what your skills are, now is the time to get help from your parents, guardians, or close relatives. Ask questions about your younger self such as what were the things you liked doing when you were growing up? What were your hobbies? What's something you were passionate about? Getting people that were around you when you were growing up to answer these questions is another way to discover things you are truly passionate about. Our parents, especially, see through us. They can easily pick out your skills because they've known all your attributes right from the very start.

Also, try to rekindle your childhood passion. As you grow up, you tend to see some of your childhood dreams as unrealistic or irrational, making you give up on considering those things. Brainstorm about all the activities you loved but had to stop pursuing because you thought they weren't worth it. You can give those activities a second chance to see if you still enjoy doing them. Think of all the important things you enjoyed doing growing up.

Consider the things you have always wanted to try.

Everyone has something they have always dreamed of doing. You have always thought of it but have never actually pursued those activities. You might have your reservations or just the fear of starting. You will never get to know if you are passionate about something until you give it a try. You may have always wanted to join the school dance group, but you fear the competitions or see the dancers as people far better than you are. The truth is, if you never give it a try, you might be unable to unleash a hidden passion there.

Open yourself to new opportunities so you can discover things you don't even know how much you like. Start by making a list of activities you have a slight interest in and figure out ways to explore them. Don't stay close-minded and not give things a try because you feel you might not be comfortable doing it or you aren't good at it. It would help if you were open-minded, so you could explore things you may be passionate about. Be open to exploring your interests; give it a try and see how things turn out.

Think deeply

Once you have discovered your hobbies, interests, dreams, and the things you enjoy doing, you might have quite a list there. Now is the time to brainstorm and figure it out. Write down all your ideas on paper and figure out your top passions. You don't need an organized list of ideas; a rough jot is okay. Everything will eventually come in handy later.

You can find a source of inspiration on your computer or anything around you and write whatever comes to your mind. There is no bad idea; it is about discovering what you truly care about.

Find a mentor in your area of interest.

Once you have been able to get the skills and activities you are certain you are genuinely passionate about, it's a good idea to find someone in your field of interest who can mentor you and expose you to the information you need to know about your area of interest. A mentor will help you navigate your interests and learn more about them. A mentor can be a teacher, coach, friend, family member, or professional. However, your mentor should be someone who shares a similar interest with you and has spent some time in the area of interest that you want to explore. Make inquiries and have meaningful conversations with them about the activity or skills you want to develop.

Tips:

Don't blindly follow your instincts. Everything requires patience, careful planning, and a great deal of commitment.

Invest time in your interests

The goal is not just to discuss activities and skills you are passionate about but also to make time to work on them passionately. You won't get a chance to develop your interests if you don't commit your time. Make time for your interests every week to learn more about them. The more you know about your skills, talents, and interests, the more you'll value them, and your passion will also grow. It takes time for your passion to grow, so you must devote your time to it. You can also find a class, or a coach related to your passion for accountability purposes. You should also get rid of time wasters from your schedule. For instance, you can spend less time on social media and more time on your passion.

Endure through challenges and failure

There will be challenges as you delve deeper into your passion. People face different challenges; even the wealthiest entrepreneurs do. I've had my fair share, but I always believed everything would work out. You may not be naturally good at an activity you are passionate about but keep working through the challenges. There is always room for improvement. Passion requires time and hard work. Dedicate your time to working hard toward your passion and treat any pitfall as a steppingstone to success. Don't give up; keep putting in your best efforts and endure through it all. While it is important to persevere, it might be time to redirect your energy elsewhere if you are no longer enjoying carrying out those activities.

WHY YOU NEED TO CONSIDER ENTREPRENEURSHIP

All successful entrepreneurs begin their careers at a young age. Many started their journey by babysitting, washing cars for families, coaching, and so on. Above all the advantages of starting your own business, the genuine value it provides cannot be measured by the financial gain. Its genuine worth lies in the value gained through experience, especially when you're a teenager.

I'm exploring entrepreneurship because I want to build a stable financial future for myself and make my mother and family proud. Also, I desire to grow into a responsible adult who is passionate about improving their community, making an impact on the world at large, and have the urge to be heard.

These are the factors that drove me to consider entrepreneurship. There are so many benefits that come with owning and operating your business at a young age. We all have dreams, desires, and plans for the future, but the question is, are you ready to take a step toward achieving those dreams?

What is an entrepreneur?

An entrepreneur is a person who starts a new business and bears most of the risks while reaping most of the benefits. The entrepreneur is frequently portrayed as a provider of brilliant ideas, products, services, and business processes.

Teen entrepreneurs are making outstanding records worldwide while perfectly managing their businesses, schooling, and other activities. It is never too soon to start your own business. Your small dreams can yield big profits if you have an excellent idea. It's all about taking the initial step by coming up with a concept, conducting research, and accepting you'll make mistakes along the way.

Entrepreneurship gives a sense of responsibility and accomplishment that will train you and make you a better adult in the future. Entrepreneurship provides incredible opportunities! You get to take charge of your life right from a young age. This is an opportunity that is worth trying out. When you become one, you open yourself up to a wide range of potential possibilities, that might be enormous depending on your goals and industry! There is so much you can achieve when you are passionate and hardworking.

Benefits of being a teen entrepreneur

#Entrepreneurial skills are lifelong abilities: One of the most significant benefits of starting a business at a young age is gaining skills like teamwork, networking, problem-solving, critical thinking, self-discipline, and so on.

Ring a brighter future: Entrepreneurship is a chance for teenagers to take care of their future. It is also a way for teenagers to develop solutions to problems through their young minds, bring about social and economic change, and accelerate long-term development.

#Responsibility: Yes, entrepreneurship is all about responsibility and then some. When you decide to become one, you accept the responsibility of becoming a valuable contribution to yourself, your community, and the world around you. Keep in mind that entrepreneurship comes with a lot of responsibility. Never consider entrepreneurship to be a one-day or once-a-year endeavor. It's a lifelong commitment to becoming a great resource in the world around you by consciously choosing to participate.

#Creativity: One of the most appealing aspects of entrepreneurship is the ability to create your vision of wealth and test the limits of your creative imagination. You get to turn your ideas into reality and see how far they can take you.

#Boost your candidacy for college admissions: One of the advantages is that your candidacy for top colleges will be enhanced. If you started a business in high school, colleges would admire you as an outgoing student. The latter will not only thrive in demand for world-class education, but all opportunities provided. You will get higher consideration if you run a business that has a significant social, charitable, or community initiative. A business effort aimed at bettering the world demonstrates that you have the potential to lead and improve the world in some way, as well as the will to achieve and the courage to try it out at a young age.

#Save toward college: Starting a business as a teenager can enable you to save money for your college education, thereby supporting your parent and protecting yourself from the negative effect of taking out a student loan. You'd be working toward having a financially stable future this way.

My clothing designs! I took pictures in my room! Just creating my vision for photo shoots in the future! Check me out!

Do you have what it takes to be a teen entrepreneur?

You keep wondering if you have what it takes to be a teen entrepreneur. Yeah, I understand the fear. However, we can never know our full capability until we try it. Entrepreneurship isn't all fun and games. I am not going to dispute that. There will be ups and downs, which is common with every business worldwide. Starting a business requires commitment and a full-time endeavor. It necessitates a great deal of dedication, time, and effort, so you must have the stomach for it.

You must also determine whether you can handle multiple responsibilities, especially starting in business. You could be your sole employee. That is, you may be the marketing officer, salesperson, receptionist, and so on, and if you aren't used to juggling various tasks, you must learn to do so if you want your company to flourish. You must also be able to find a way to manage your academics, your business, social activities, family time, and your personal time. There must be a balance between schoolwork, your business, things you love to do, and making good memories of your teenage years.

To stand out as an entrepreneur, you must: Be passionate about your business.

Be humble and willing to learn.

Be focused and diligent.

Be an excellent marketer and salesperson, as well as be patient.

Have excellent people and resource management skills.

Be truthful.

Have foresight and hindsight.

Be a good leader.

Have you decided to be a teen entrepreneur? Here are a few steps to follow to begin your journey into entrepreneurship:

Set your mind up for success

We often find it difficult to accept that running a teen business is possible. This may be because you've mostly heard of it but have never seen anyone around you doing it. Sadly, only a few schools provide entrepreneurship lessons, and most teenagers do not know many business owners or successful entrepreneurs. Therefore, you have no one to guide you on your journey to success.

As a result, the best thing you can do is train your mind to think positively. To learn as much as possible, you will need to research successful entrepreneurs and discover what they did to get to where they are today. Look at successful teen entrepreneurs doing well. There is quite a list if you run a

Google search. This should motivate you to set your mind up for success in your journey to entrepreneurship.

Explore the success stories of those who have and are achieving and surround yourself with greatness and success from young individuals who are making a difference. You'll discover that they don't just provide ideas and tactics for growing your business, but they also keep you encouraged and eager to keep going. Find at least one successful person in your prospective industry to whom you can look up. Create a thriving atmosphere for yourself by surrounding yourself with individuals who aspire to be. Read the right books, research biographies, and autobiographies of successful entrepreneurs who started as teens. This will help you develop your entrepreneurial skills.

Stay away from the crowd. You are concerned that most people your age want to go to school and have fun. It is a choice to stand out like other successful teen entrepreneurs who decided to create something special for themselves while still in high school to have a sustainable future. So, if you do everything your buddies do, such as lying around, partying on weekends, and playing video games, you'll end up like most people. Standing out as a teen entrepreneur doesn't mean you'll live a boring life. This just balances your time because you have more responsibility than your peers.

If necessary, obtain the required experience.

It's all about offering and adding value to the business. A common problem for young people is the lack of sufficient experience to deliver the much-needed value that a service or product should have. So, how do you get around it? Acquire experience. Whether you work for someone else or volunteer at events, you'll need additional expertise to bring value to your future consumers. You might have an advantage if one of your parent or guardians run their own business; all you must do is be patient and learn.

Also, while learning from your own mistakes can be beneficial, learning from other people's mistakes is even better. You can read about and speak to other entrepreneurs about their mistakes and then try to avoid making the same mistakes.

Make sure the right folks surround you.

Your mindset, as well as the way you act and feel, will be shaped by the people you interact with that surround you.

Keep an eye out for and surround yourself with people living and exemplifying the life you desire.

They may not always tell you what you want to hear, but they will tell you what you need to know in order to advance in your life. Spend time with people who ask questions, have lofty dreams, and work tirelessly. They will help you to be more inspired and motivated in your objectives. Keep your distance from negative people. Mom mostly inspires me. Her positivity and strong will motivated me to become who I am today.

It will be stressful for you if you do not enjoy the business you want to build.

Take risks and confront your fears.

Even though starting a business is risky, you must take more risks to succeed in your industry. Being fearful of taking risks is not a prescription for success. Take measured risks when it's time to take your business to the next level. It's important to stress, however, that taking risks is not the same as just following your intuition and jumping to a conclusion without much consideration.

To back up your decision, you must conduct thorough research. Also, as a young entrepreneur, you will have some anxieties; nonetheless, avoiding them is never the best option.

When you face your fears, they will become less complex and smaller. Fears that startups have include not knowing where to begin, not being a professional, being labeled a fanatic for having radical ideas, not being able to acquire startup money, not attracting clients, and so on.

Set goals

Set goals that will allow you to assess your progress in building your business regularly. That will determine whether you are doing well or need to make changes to improve your business. Your goal should include short-term, medium-term, and long-term objectives. Make sure your goals are measured regularly and are reachable, reasonable, and time phased. If feasible, go above and beyond the goals you've set for yourself and your company.

BUSINESS IDEA

You have decided to go into entrepreneurship, but now you are stuck because you don't know what kind of business to go into. This stage is a critical one that must be given proper attention. It is essential to incorporate quality attributes to make your business idea effective. People often have an idea for a business but will not go through the steps necessary to make it viable and suitable for the market. Various factors make a business idea more likely to succeed. Here are some of the characteristics of a good business idea to improve your chances of success while developing your business idea:

A good business idea must:

Be scalable: Scalability is one of the most significant aspects of a solid business idea. This enables the business to increase in status. A scalable business model will allow your company to increase its profits and sales over time without any new inputs or costs. You can have a good business idea but achieving success will be difficult if it is not scalable.

Solve a problem: All outstanding ideas must be able to solve a problem that potential consumers will appreciate. The finished result should be logical and user-friendly, making it simple to comprehend.

Have a target audience: When creating a business idea, you must have prospective customers. Who will be your customers? Who are those that need your products or services? Before creating an idea, you should know your target audience.

Have an existing market: If there is a market for your business idea, there are many good businesses to start. To confirm that your business idea has a need, conduct extensive surveys and collect data to determine whether the business can bring value to the people.

Be sustainable: To succeed, your business idea needs to be sustainable. This means that you must have access to limitless resources. One of the leading causes of business failure is the scarcity of essential resources. Also, your business idea must have a vision. It will be challenging our daily operations without a compelling vision, leaving the company susceptible to failure.

Be profitable: You must be able to predict if your business idea will be profitable. With the help of a financial projection, you should be able to estimate when you will make your first profit. This is a solid indicator of the viability of your business concepts. If the estimate shows that the business will not be profitable, you might have to start brainstorming new business ideas.

Be unique: This doesn't mean your business idea will not be similar to an existing business, but that you must be able to stand out and offer something unique that will set you apart from your competitors.

Ways to come up with a business idea.

Explore your passions and talents

If you have identified your passion, unique talent, or acquired skill, you're already a step ahead in the game. I love the era we are in now. The internet has made it possible for young minds to showcase their unique talents, skills, and passions to the world. There are many ways to earn money from the internet, including TikTok, YouTube, indie podcasts, and many others. If you have a special skill or talents, you can create a business idea around them. For instance, if you hold good conversations, debates and have so much to share with the world, you can go into podcasting or start a YouTube channel about the topics you love to discuss. You can write your book or work as a freelance writer if you have excellent writing skills.

An excellent way to create a business idea is to turn your skills, talents, hobbies, and passions into a successful business idea. Once you have a skill or talent, creating a business idea becomes more effortless. Make sure your business idea can solve a problem, entertain people, or provide a service. If the prospect of establishing your business idea scares you, the best place to start is with something you are already familiar with.

This way, it won't feel like a challenging task, and you will be able to enjoy starting and building the business. However, keep in mind how you'll feel if things work out. You may find that things become less pleasurable if you are forced to begin doing your passion for meeting consumer demands or paying the bills. Or perhaps you simply need a new interest!

Establish a new product or service

I established a clothing line because I was aware of the bullying by the kids around me. I aim to spread positivity and raise the self-esteem of those around me. The key to creating a business idea around creating a product or service is identifying a problem and providing a solution. My way of providing a solution to the problem around me was to increase positivity, which is the aim of my clothing line.

Examples of business ideas for teenagers

It is better to base your business ideas on something you enjoy doing or a problem you wish to solve. However, I want to provide a list of ideas based on research and what other teenagers are thriving off. The best approach is to choose a business idea that suits your personality. Keep in mind that these are just possibilities of things you can explore based on your interests and skills.

Art and design business ideas

Graphic design: The designs we see in publications, websites, physical cards, business logos, and other mediums is known as graphic design. This business is most suitable for people who are artistically inclined. You can design logos, text, images, wedding invitations, website images, animations, or any other type of graphic art. To get started, you will need a skill you can easily access by watching a few YouTube videos. Materials required are computer and graphic design tools like Adobe. Once you've honed your skills, you can launch your business by designing logos for your school, friends, and family to build a strong portfolio. Once you have mastered this, you can start connecting with clients through various freelancing platforms or find clients around you.

Photography: If you love to take good pictures and help people remember important events in their lives, or if you enjoy taking quality pictures of nature, you can consider going into the photography business. To get started, you will need some training and experience. You will also need a quality camera, computer, lighting equipment, and editing software.

Your potential earnings will increase as your skills improve, giving your business more exposure, especially when you start shooting for significant events such as weddings or other special occasions.

Illustration business: For talented and artistic teens, starting an illustration business is a brilliant way to make money. Illustrating books, creating cartoon characters, and making storyboards are all possibilities. Being up to date on digital illustration technologies is critical in this sector. You may begin by making unique gifts for friends and family or generating graphics for school newspapers and local magazines. Your earning potential will increase as your reputation and portfolio improve.

Make-up artist business: Anyone who enjoys interacting with people and has exceptional make-up application skills can find success as a make-up artist. Using social media to establish a name for oneself can be highly beneficial. You might start by doing your friends' make-up for events like homecoming to create your portfolio. This is a wonderful business for a teenager to start. If you establish a brand among your friends early on, your clients will return to your services for the rest of their lives.

Craft business ideas

Soap-making business: Do you enjoy working with your hands? Starting a soap-making business is an excellent idea. Anyone can learn how to make soap but producing high-quality soap takes time and consistent practice. Buying raw materials, mixing and creating fragrances, making the soap, and selling the soap are all part of operating a soap-making business. You can then establish an online market when you have a strong portfolio.

Sewing business: A sewing business is a great business idea if you have sewing skills. This flexible business is ideal for young individuals who are especially intrigued by the latest fashion trends. Your customer base and earning capacity will increase as your brand grows.

E-commerce and social media business ideas

Online reseller: Starting an online reseller business is also an excellent idea. Teens who wish to earn money while exploring their entrepreneurial spirit can consider starting an online reseller business. You can buy items such as clothes, souvenirs, collectibles, and so on from local retailers and resell them on your website or eBay.

Social media marketing: If you're fascinated by how social media platforms work and enjoy communicating with large numbers of people, social media marketing could be a lucrative venture for you. You can explore various social media platforms, such as Facebook, Instagram, Twitter, TikTok, Snapchat, etc. However, having an account on these channels isn't enough. To maintain a consistent level of engagement with your followers, you must post content regularly. It also doesn't have to be a lot of content! Building a solid account will enable you to take on brand and social media influencers' jobs from various businesses once they are assured you have a large engagement.

Writing and publishing business ideas.

Writing children's books: Starting a children's book business could be a good fit if you love writing, painting, or telling stories. Children's books have consistently sold more copies than adult books due to the amount of reading that children do compared to adults. Fortunately, many self-publishing platforms are available now that will save you startup costs compared to traditional publishing.

Freelance writing services: Teens have access to a myriad of freelance writing options such as books, articles, blog posts, music, and lyrics, among several others. Companies are releasing more material to reach consumers worldwide from various perspectives, thanks to the internet's ever-expanding reach. Anyone interested in pursuing a writing career should take advantage of this opportunity to establish a portfolio. Other services include proofreading, editing, book design, transcription, etc.

Tip: "Doubting yourself is normal. Letting it stop you is a choice."- Mel Robbins

Validating Your Business Idea

Note that the ideas above are only suggestions. Conducting your market research will allow you to identify and fine-tune the type of adolescent business you want to establish. However, don't believe it'll be simple to run because it's a teen business.

You must be polite, dependable, and punctual. You should deliver services as promised and ensure that customers are satisfied with the outcome. This will aid in developing your brand and may result in positive word-of-mouth and increased sales.

Don't limit yourself to the ideas listed above in this book alone. The truth is that business ideas are endless; every day, people keep developing new ideas. Entrepreneurship comes with a wide range of several ideas and opportunities. It is possible to have a very distinct idea. Don't be scared to pursue your dreams.

Legitimize your business idea

Once you have successfully decided on your business idea and come to the final decision on the business you want to start, now is the time to do some research.

Market research

Conducting research is the most critical step in launching a business. It is fine to take as much time as you want at this stage. It is entirely dependent on how much time you have set aside for research. Note that the more research you do on the front end, the more productive your business will be on the back end.

You should learn everything you can. The more you know, the easier it will be to see a trend or a need that your small business can meet. Analyzing one idea can sometimes lead to another that is more viable or easier to execute.

Why market research is essential

Over-enthusiasm and a lack of knowledge about a new business is a recipe for failure. People who believe they are ready to start a business frequently make the error of jumping into initiatives without first conducting research. They then have a nasty revelation when they understand what they've gotten into.

Before jumping in with both feet, every aspiring entrepreneur should perform considerable research. Most new business owners learn by trial and error, yet it's impossible to avoid conducting research.

Market research doesn't have to be complex. With the help of the internet, you can easily have enough research done. Read books that will assist you in gaining deep knowledge about the business you are building. This knowledge will help you better understand the business and guide you through potential pitfalls.

Research your competitors

Research who your competitors are and the demand for the product or service you've chosen. When conducting your research, keep in mind to be specific. Even if your product or service is unique, there can still be a business that offers something similar or uses similar approaches to meet the same customers' needs. To clearly understand why customers, choose one product or service over another, you must consider your competition.

Spend some time on the internet gathering preliminary information about the competitors and the marketplace. Try a quick Google search for "home cleaners near me" and see what comes up. Based on the findings, you'll know how common the business idea is and who your competitors are.

When you've figured out who your competitors are, it is okay to contact them. They may be an excellent resource for learning more about what to anticipate and the market's genuine needs.

Research your target audience

Identify who your product or service will benefit. To ensure the success of your business, figure out the audience that will benefit the most from your product or service. The more you know about your customers, the more confident you can be in your business' success. It is also important to consider your target demographics, such as age, gender, location, race, etc.

Make a basic list of prospective customers and include as much information as possible. For instance, you could say that your consumers will be women of diverse colors who desire to express their power and self-esteem. When defining your audience, there is no such thing as too much information!

Survey your target audience to determine whether they would utilize your product or service. Also, make a lot of inquiries to establish the value of your product about your target demographic.

Consider your options for funding.

If you cannot fund your business' start-up with the money you saved, you will need to find someone who can assist you with financing. Before approaching a parent, guardian, or another adult for assistance, be sure you have a plan for how much money you'll need, how you'll spend it, and how you'll repay any borrowed money.

Make a simple yet thorough budget for your business.

Determine how much money you have and how much more you'll need based on your budget.

Describe your plans for raising funds and repaying investors.

Prospective investors should review your business plan as well as your budget.

Bank accounts and business credit

People under eighteen are officially deemed minors, meaning you won't be able to open a company bank account. It also implies that you won't be able to borrow money or use a credit card, and you will be required to find another way to fund your business. This might be:

- Obtaining a loan from a family member to help you support your business.

- Forming a partnership with an adult who is legally entitled to receive financing.

- Enterprise funds, trusts, and agencies that provide grants or cash payouts.

Choose a name for your business.

Remember that your company's name will give your customers a first impression. The name should reflect the practical use of your goods or services for your customers.

Signify your uniqueness from competitors and express your company's concept.

Consider a variety of names for your product or service, keeping in mind that the more your name conveys about your business to people, the less work it will require you to describe it.

Once you've decided on a name, check to see whether it's already been taken by another brand or company. You will most likely be able to obtain this information by conducting a few basic online searches. There are excellent software you can use online that are free. For example, you can use Thomas Register as a resource tool for locating unregistered trademarks.

Before deciding on a name, talk to your friends and relatives. Ask them to write down what comes to mind immediately when they hear your company's name.

If required, make changes to the name according to the input you've received.

Once you have chosen a name, it is important to trademark your business name. You don't want to build a name to a point where someone else is already using it before you can trademark it.

Register your business

You may be required to register your business as it grows and becomes more than just a passion. Out of all the decisions you make in forming your business, this might be the one relating most to taxes. Your business' legal structure impacts how much you are to pay in taxes, the amount of paperwork required, the personal liability you face, and your ability to raise funds.

Moreover, you will need to secure various federal and state licenses and permits to conduct your business legally. Seek the help of a parent, legal guardian, or another responsible adult to establish whether your company must be registered. With the help of my mom, I was able to register my business with the secretary of state in Louisiana as an LLC.

Before registering a business, you should know the different business entities and choose the one that best fits your business.

Understanding the legal components of a business will aid you in deciding what sort of business to start. Most enterprises are set up in the following manners:

- ❖ Sole proprietorship

- Partnership
- Limited liability Company (LLC)
- For-profit corporation
- Non-profit corporation (not-for-profit)

Sole proprietorship

The most popular type of business is a sole proprietorship. In the United States, at least 80% of small firms are operated as "single proprietorships." Because it is the easiest and simplest structure to establish and operate, most small firms are sole proprietorships. As a result, for young entrepreneurs, starting as a sole proprietor makes perfect sense.

A sole proprietorship is a business owned and operated by one individual. However, staff may be present. You and your business are the same in a sole proprietorship. You are the business!

Starting a firm as a sole proprietor might also be less expensive. Unlike an LLC or a Corporation, a Sole Proprietorship can be formed quickly.

Advantages of a sole proprietorship

The benefit of starting a business as a sole proprietor is that you have total control and decision-making authority over the company; you own it and may sell it whenever you choose.

A sole proprietorship has low legal fees and few formal business regulations. The owner pays taxes on business income as part of his or her individual income tax payments.

The setback of a sole proprietorship

One of the disadvantages of a sole proprietorship is that the business' debts and liabilities can be held against the sole proprietor personally. Because you and your business are one, if you are sued, the court has the authority to seek personal property – such as your home, car, or equipment – to pay off your business debts.

This risk also applies to any liabilities incurred due to actions taken by company workers. The sole owner is responsible for all duties and company choices, and investors rarely invest in sole proprietorships.

Another disadvantage of a sole proprietorship is that your tax return may be scrutinized more closely, possibly leading to an audit by the Internal Revenue Service (IRS.gov).

Partnership

A partnership is formed when two or more people team up to run a business. Everyone is involved in the business, and the business, like a sole proprietorship, is inextricably linked to these members; they jointly own it. This has significant legal ramifications because the activities of one partner on behalf of the company influence the other partners as well.

A partnership is a business held by two or more people who haven't filed papers to form a corporation or a limited liability company (LLC). Except for the standard registration requirements for all new firms, no paperwork is required to register a partnership. When you start a business with another person, the arrangement begins. Individual taxes are paid in alliances, depending on a share of the business' profit or loss. The partnership is legally terminated when one of the partners dies. If the correct arrangements were established in the Partnership agreement, the business might be able to continue.

Sole proprietorships and partnerships are appropriate for businesses where personal responsibility isn't a significant concern, such as a small service business where you're unlikely to be sued and won't be borrowing much money for inventory or other expenses.

Limited Liability Corporations (LLC)

A limited liability company (LLC) is a legal entity that combines various beneficial features for a specific type of business. A Limited Liability Company (LLC) combines the elements of a corporation and a partnership, providing liability protection to its owners (which is often reserved for corporations) and simplifying taxes by transferring profits and losses to the owners (like a Partnership).

"Articles of Organization" are filed with the Secretary of State to incorporate a limited liability company. Many other requirements could be put in the articles and perhaps should be. Creating an LLC is a simple process. The decision of whether to form an LLC is a difficult one. The Corporations Division advises filers to get competent legal business assistance before and after creation to ensure that the filer's goals and intents are accomplished, and those legal requirements are completed.

Advantages of limited liability corporations

Personal liability protection for members; no need to meet the requirements and formalities of a corporation to maintain business status.

Members can draw up their contract, allowing flexibility in management and responsibilities and greater flexibility in allocating income to members than in a corporation.

Investors will be interested in investing in an LLC rather than a sole proprietorship.

Corporations

Corporations and LLCs make sense for business owners who are concerned about being sued by customers or clients, who are concerned about accumulating a large number of business debts, or who have a significant number of personal assets they want to shield from business creditors. The fact that a corporation is a separate legal and tax entity from the people who own, control, and manage it distinguishes it from all other forms of enterprises.

Due to the separate status, a corporation's owners do not use their personal tax returns to pay taxes on corporate profits; instead, the corporation pays these taxes. Only the money they receive from the corporation in the form of salary, bonuses, and other benefits is subject to personal income tax.

Limited liability companies (LLCs) are similar to corporations in limiting personal liability for corporate debts and claims. LLCs, on the other hand, are more like partnerships when it comes to taxes. On their personal tax returns, LLC owners pay taxes on their part of the corporate income.

Not-for-profit corporations

A charitable, educational, religious, literary, or scientific aim is carried out by a non-profit corporation. Grant money from the public and private sectors, as well as donations from individuals and businesses, can help a non-profit obtain much needed funding.

Many non-profit organizations ask for funds after obtaining their 501(c) (3) status. A 501(c) (3) organization or group will be exempt from paying taxes on any gifts made to a non-profit. However, the IRS closely monitors this money, making your non-profit even more scrutinized. Because of the services they provide to society, the federal and state governments do not usually tax non-profit corporations on their money connected to their non-profit mission.

BUSINESS BRANDING

This section is yet another essential aspect of your business setup because branding ensures that the image of your business in the heads of consumers is identical to the image you want them to have. Expectations are what brands are. Building a brand requires concentration, passion, perseverance, and diligence. Furthermore, brand growth necessitates effort and dedication. The payback, and it's a significant one, is that strong brands are essential for personal and business success.

Customers will remember your brand for good or bad. Branding is the process of forming correct and aligned consumer thoughts and perceptions with what you want your brand to be.

What does a brand do?

Consumer trust and emotional relationships are built by brands. As a result, they develop consumer-product relationships that resist price competition, outperform new competitor offers, and even overcome rare breaches in product or service quality. Great brands aren't merely well-known or well-respected. They are adored.

Benefits of branding

Look forward to receiving the following benefits as your brand grows in strength and loyalty in your market sector.

Brands make it easier to sell. People like to buy from businesses they recognize and believe in. Brands provide that certainty. Whether selling items to customers, providing freelance or consulting services to clients, or providing other services, a brand establishes a positive perception of your unique and significant proposition before you even offer your sales pitch. Customers recognize what you stand for and what distinctive value they can count on you to give when they are aware of your brand and its unique and positive features. As a result, when it's time to sell, brand owners can focus on the customer's wants and needs because they don't have to explain themselves.

You must create a case for the value you give every time you get ready to make a sale if you don't have positive brand awareness. Those without solid brands are still introducing themselves while brand owners are completing the deal.

1. Brand recognition

In its most basic form, business branding produces an indelible impact on customers' minds. Building a business brand might be pretty challenging, but it does entail developing consumer recognition. Brand recognition may take many forms, with internet exposure quickly rising to the top of the list of the most effective ways to create a lasting impression on customers.

2. Brands enhance the chances of a business' survival.

New businesses and services are being established at an extraordinary speed. Only those who enter the market with an established brand or can quickly construct a brand name will be able to capture public knowledge, understanding, and preference in time to survive.

3. Brands influence consumers' purchasing decisions.

Consumers can shop and buy without regard to their location in recent times. The internet and other at-home purchasing options provide global access to any product from any location. Consumers can find and select products with familiar names and guarantees with a few clicks or keystrokes. Brands rule in this vast marketplace, and no-name products rarely make it.

4. Personal branding allows you to highlight your unique abilities.

Building a solid personal brand is founded on the distinct abilities that set you apart from the competition. Your unique combination of professional experience, personality, life experience, and communication abilities is impressive. Even though many individuals have similar characteristics, talents, and experiences, this is the case. People will notice your distinctiveness when you spend time and money on personal branding.

5. You gain more self-assurance.

You will notice a significant increase in self-confidence as you develop your brand's image and highlight your strengths and skillsets. As you see your brand grow and extend, as well as the excellent feedback from friends, family, mentors, and senior peers in your field, you'll find yourself growing increasingly self-assured.

Identifying your brand purpose

You need your brand to have a purpose that strongly matches the one that your target audience will have in life. You'll learn what a brand's purpose is, the different sorts of brand purposes, how they might help your business, and how they affect how you plan for your brand's existence, growth, and development. Because each brand is distinct, the aim of each one will differ. It's not only about selling stuff; it's also about selling an experience and a purpose. Essentially, the goal of your brand is similar to that of a real person. It's usually based on a subject that the company is passionate about and wants to assist in its business operations. Typically, a brand's mission will focus on what it can do for its customers rather than just selling products or services.

Your brand must have a meaning: Your brand has to have importance! Consider what you want your business to symbolize and combine it with your business name. What does my brand have to offer? What needs does my brand meet? Consider these questions and write down the significance of your brand. Remember, the descriptive words you write down should leave an unforgettable impression on your customers.

Determine the industry niche in which you operate, and then create terms that set you apart from your competition. You must understand everything there is to know about your target consumer group, and how your products and services address their primary needs.

Building Your Brand Identity Display Fonts:

These are in another category altogether. They are diverse in form. Every display font has a unique feature, such as a unique letter form, outlines, shadowing, or a more artistic/hand-drawn edge. Consider Metallica's lightning bolt font if you want to make a dramatic statement and establish a memorable brand identity.

Select your fonts intelligently because the typography you use will speak volumes about your brand.

Brand color

Color is yet another vital element of your branding process. They have a strong and immediate effect and quickly convey important messages. Your business branding color will strongly impact your various marketing assets, from how your website is designed to your logo, business cards, social media accounts, etc. Setting up a consistent brand color across all your business platforms will result in a unified look and bring a feel to your business, making it easily recognizable and memorable.

How to choose your brand color

Brand colors are a collection or palette of colors that are used in representing a business. The consistent and deliberate use of brand colors can help to increase brand awareness and recognition. Brand colors are mainly applied to a business' logo, social media channels, website color scheme, print, digital ads, business card design, etc. For brick-and-mortar businesses, the brand colors can be used for the store design, employee uniforms, packaging design, and more.

According to the colors combined with, and context and cultural meanings, colors can represent different things. However, there are distinct industry-specific color patterns. Here's a quick summary of standard brand colors to help you choose the proper color palette for your business:

Fashion and beauty: Black is generally associated with refinement and luxury, whereas warm hues like red, orange and pink are associated with passion, confidence, and excitement in the fashion and beauty industry.

Food: Most food and restaurant businesses use warm colors like red, orange, and yellow to capture attention and induce appetite. Other food products use green to emphasize a connection to health and well-being, whereas, sweets and desserts use blue and pink.

Health and wellness: Blue is commonly used in the health and wellness industry to represent cleanliness, integrity, and accountability. Green, represents nature and wholesomeness, and orange, which can conjure up images of life and energy, are two more common choices.

High-tech: Blue is a popular choice for tech organizations because it represents reliability, knowledge, and efficiency. Orange, welcoming and enthusiastic, and purple, which represents quality and creativity, are two other hues to consider.

Form, shape, and imagery

The shapes you use in your logo, packaging, business cards, and other elements can communicate much about your business. Round shapes, for example, evoke thoughts of camaraderie and unity along with some warmth and fuzzy feeling, whereas sharper, straight-edged shapes evoke feelings of effectiveness and dependability.

Here's how different shapes might influence your brand's identity:

Round shapes: Round shapes such as circles, ovals, and ellipses are all about feeling good. Brands with round shapes might evoke feelings of connection, harmony, and love. The curved edges have a feminine feel to them.

Shapes with straight edges: Squares, rectangles, and triangles evoke feelings of strength and competence. The consecutive lines convey solidity and reliability but be careful.

If the forms aren't toned out with something exciting, such as vibrant colors, they can feel cold and fail to engage with your audience.

Vertical lines imply masculinity and strength, while horizontal lines imply calm and peaceful vibes.

The right imagery, when employed correctly, can enhance a customer's commitment to your business. Images form the aesthetic of your brand. These images can be found on Facebook, Instagram, websites, and print advertisement, among other places. These photos are more than just graphics; they are an opportunity to speak with your prospective customer. They might be modern or old, basic or sophisticated, elegant or rough. You must source pictures your audience will connect with to find the perfect images.

Knowing these brand identity elements before working with a graphic designer, can get the accurate image you want your brand to portray and make your audience see you just the way you want!

Getting your brand identity ready

It is the perfect time to start with your designer on making your brand identity a reality and express who you are as a brand. Your existing design resources will be used in your marketing, once defined successfully define the basic elements of your brand identity as discussed above. Any number of elements can be used in your design to express your brand identity. However, depending on your business niche, some elements may be more significant than others when making your design. For instance, a digital marketing agency will focus more on the website and social media platforms, whereas a restaurant will focus more on the physical appearance, packaging, and menu.

Aspects of your brand identity

Logo

Your logo is the rock of your brand's identity. While working with your graphic designer, make sure that your logo checks all the boxes:

Effectively communicates the essence of your brand and the value you provide.

Is aesthetically attractive: simplicity, cleanliness, and a lack of clutter will be perfect!

You don't want your logo to become outdated in no time.

Plays by the rules of your industry—and if you deviate, do so on purpose.

Makes a lasting impression on your potential audience.

BUILDING A BUSINESS WEBSITE

A business without a digital presence may not survive. No matter where you are running your business, it is essential to have a business website. Customers use the internet for product research to determine where a business is located and its operating hours. A well-designed website can give you a competitive advantage in your industry and help you develop your business quickly and affordably.

The great part is that building a business website doesn't have to be complex. Once you have a computer and internet, you can quickly build your website with website builders like Shopify, enabling you to develop your business website without coding. Website design software has advanced to the point where anyone can use it.

Steps to building a business website

These are step-by-step guidelines to follow when building a business website.

Step one: Determine the focus of your website

You can build a website without a focus. Businesses' websites are created for different goals. The goal might be to provide basic information about your business, an eCommerce store to sell your products, a platform to sell your services or a blog. You must define the goal and the main focus of your website before getting started at all. It is important to state what your brand does.

A website is typically used to provide basic information about your business or as a straight e-commerce platform.

Whatever your business website's goal, you must focus on creating a user-friendly interface that users will easily navigate through. No one wants to engage with a website that is complex and difficult to navigate. Make sure that whatever the focus of your website is, it must be user-friendly to ensure customer engagement and satisfaction.

Step two: Choose a website builder

A website builder is the quickest way to develop a business website. With minimal work or technical knowledge, an easy-to-use website builder will make setting up your business website faster. These tools benefit new business owners since they make it simple to create a website.

I would recommend using Shopify as your website builder. I used it to set up my brand website, which is excellent.

Step three: Choose your domain name

The domain name is one of the essential aspects of any website. It's the link you'll send to current and new customers and promote on social media. Keep it simple, and avoid abbreviations, acronyms, and numerals if possible, to avoid customer confusion. When you've decided on a domain name, you'll need to check for availability and purchase it immediately. A few well-known domain registrars include:

- Domain.com
- GoDaddy
- Squarespace
- Wix

Step four: Build your pages

A standard website is more than just a page with text on it. You should have different pages focused on other areas of your business, such as a complete catalog of your products or services, a blog section for trendy updates, a section about the business, etc. In general, your overall website design pages should each contribute to the focus and goals of your business.

A call-to-action must include, for instance, buy now, contact us, or sign up.

The following are standard pages that you should include on your website:

Homepage: This is your website's main page. This page should be able to tell visitors who you are and the products or services you offer. Make a positive first impression on visitors or potential customers by using the homepage to direct them to specific actions on your website.

Product or service page: Depending on the product you are selling; you can create a product or service page where you describe your product and encourage customers to buy if necessary.

Contact us page: This allows customers to contact you with any questions. You can provide various contact options or point folks to an FAQ. Create a contact form for users to fill out with their information and send a message to your customer service team.

FAQ page: Here, you can respond to frequently asked questions about your brand. It's an excellent method to promote self-service and free up customer support resources.

About us: Create a page that outlines your business concept and recounts your story. An About page helps visitors connect with your brand and establishes confidence. You can also include links to your social media profiles.

Policy page: Regardless of your business type, certain legal policies must be followed. For instance, you must include a refund and shipping policy.

Pictures: Include high-quality images of your products or concepts that convey information about your services. Adding low-quality photos will not attract visitors and won't promote sales. You can also include quality pictures of yourself to gain customers' trust.

Step five: establish a payment method (if applicable)

While this step isn't required for all business websites, those who wish to allow clients to pay online or whose business needs customers to pay online. You must connect electronic payment systems with your sites. A shopping cart or e-commerce link is available from many web hosts.

Step six: Test and publish your website

Before publishing your website, you must test it and ensure it works perfectly before going live. Make sure you try the website on major browsers such as Firefox, Google Chrome, Internet Explorer, Safari, etc. Ensure the site works well, each page is visible, the links are correct, and the template looks great. You don't have to rush the testing period. It takes time, but the time you invest now will save you from losing customers due to poor site functionality.

Also, check to ensure your website looks great and functions well across every mobile device, such as smartphones, tablets, and computers.

Step seven: Market your website on social media

Once your business website is live, it is time to start marketing to drive sales. The best approach to enhancing your audience and informing people of the new things going on with your brand is to use social media platforms such as Instagram, Facebook, Twitter, LinkedIn, Pinterest, etc. Once your website is live, let your social media followers know about it, but make sure you keep the post real and non-promotional.

Also, include links to your social media business pages on your website.

Step eight: Make a search engine optimization investment (SEO).

To get a targeted audience and direct potential leads to your business website, you should consider uploading your website to major search engines and implementing a solid SEO strategy across your website. You should include relevant title tags, meta descriptions, and Uniform Resources identifiers (URLs) for your business and brand, which will enable you to rank higher in search engines for the products or services you are offering.

From the start of setting up your website, make sure you include relevant keywords for your products and focus on search engine optimization.

While building your website, take note of the following points to boost your rank:

Choose the appropriate keywords: Choose keywords that are related to your brand and that your targeted audience is looking for when doing an internet search.

Publish new material: Regularly posting to a blog, adding to your website, and upgrading your content indicate to search engines that your site is relevant to the keywords you've picked.

Choose issues that are both relevant to your business and exciting for your market.

Step nine: maintain your website.

Constantly update new products and deals, blog posts on trendy happenings in your niche, etc.

Establishing a business website is a low-cost investment that can help you create trust and reach a more extensive consumer base. You'll be able to reach a larger customer base, and there is nothing like being invisible to current and potential customers. Make sure you keep your website updated with new, current, and unique materials, and timely responses to technological concerns.

MARKETING YOUR BUSINESS

When starting your business idea or concept, it is vital to include how you will advertise your brand. You would have seen many brands advertising their brands on TV, magazines, radio, posters, etc.

Entrepreneurs have long used billboards, flyers, newsletters, and brochures to keep old customers informed and recruit new ones. Note that you can sorely run a business, but not without a customer. Before any customer becomes your customer or client, they are referred to as potential or prospective customers. Your marketing skills mainly attract customers. Getting customers, keeping them, and growing their number will make your business successful.

The Acadiana Advocate Interview!

THE ACADIANA ADVOCATE

Be You: This young entrepreneur is following her dreams and inspiring others along the way

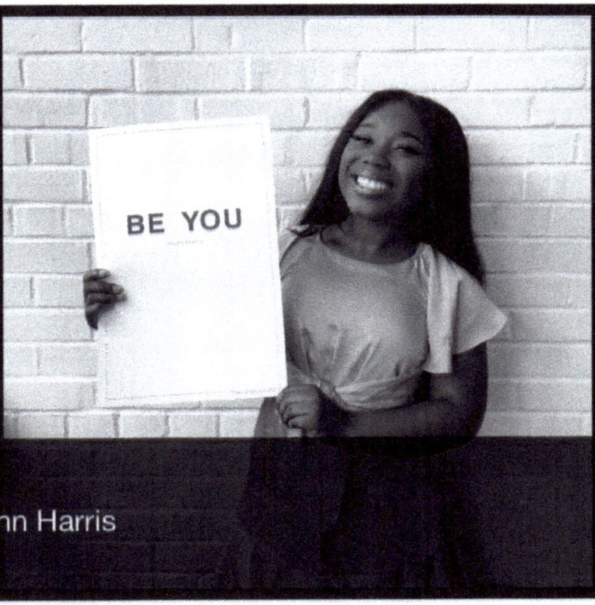

Asia'Lynn Harris

BY AILEEN BENNETT | Contributing writer

Jun 10, 2021 - 10:34 am

Asia'Lynn Harris is an entrepreneur with two fashion lines to her name — and she about to start her senior year in high school. Her two clothing brands A'cole and Polished (my world my way) are her way of spreading positivity. She wants everyone to know that there is more out there for them, and to go after your dreams and

The Daily Advertiser Interviewing me at my home!

Ranking SEC defensive backs entering the 2021 season

SPORTS, 1B

THE DAILY ADVERTISER

WE ARE ACADIANA SINCE 1865 • TUESDAY, JULY 6, 2021 • PART OF THE USA TODAY NETWORK

Fashioning a dream

Asia'Lynn Harris, a 17-year-old entrepreneur and creator of two clothing lines, started Polished My World My Way in 2012 with the goal of spreading positivity among her peers at school and students everywhere.
PHOTOS BY SCOTT CLAUSE/THE ADVERTISER

Abbeville teen balances school, cheer and the two clothing brands she created

Leigh Guidry Lafayette Daily Advertiser | USA TODAY NETWORK

Asia'Lynn Harris, 17, has to fit a lot in a day. With cheer practice and her summer job at a local tutoring center, she would be busy enough, but that's just brushing the surface. • The rising Abbeville High senior also is completing online courses in Rowan University's Think Like An Entrepreneur virtual summer academy and putting what she's learning into practice in real time with her two clothing brands • "It's a lot to manage," she admits. "I keep up with it. It gets hectic sometimes. When I'm not busy I'm bored."

See TEEN, Page 3A

Asia'Lynn Harris' love for fashion and pageantry played a part in creating a clothing business, but fashion also was a strategic business choice for her.

Officials urge COVID-19 vaccinations as variant spreads in US

Melissa Brown Montgomery Advertiser
USA TODAY NETWORK

When Montgomery pulmonologist Dr. David Thrasher arranged to send a COVID-19 sample for variant testing at a state lab on Thursday, he knew it might contain one of just a few dozen delta variant cases identified in Alabama.

But Thrasher thinks the 27 delta cases identified in the state in recent weeks are just the tip of the iceberg, as COVID-19 cases are once again on the rise in the U.S. even as the country attempts to return to normalcy.

"There's probably a lot more [delta cases] than we know of," Thrasher said. "I predict it will be the dominant starting soon in the U.S. ... We're still a very low vaccinated state and the delta is hitting people younger. The ones in the hospital, the ones I'm treating outpatient now, almost all of them are in their 40s, in their 50s."

Though COVID-19 cases and hospitalizations have plummeted since a winter surge, the national weekly average of cases rose 10% this week, according to a Centers for Disease Control and Prevention briefing. The delta variant, considered to be a much more contagious version of the virus, is increasingly circulating through the country.

While early data suggests the current COVID-19 vaccinations on the market offer protection against the new variant, experts warn the variant could lead to a new surge in communities with low vaccination rates. The South, which continues to trail the rest of the nation in vaccination rates and has higher rates of at-risk populations, is particularly at risk.

Less than 40% of people in Alabama, Mississippi, Georgia, Louisiana and Tennessee have been fully vaccinated. Some fare better in partial vaccination coverage, except in Alabama, Mississippi and Louisiana, where less than 40% of the population have got-

Marketing tools needed to run a business

Note that the marketing tools you go for depending on your business type. Note that all these tools may not apply to your business type.

Business card

Aside from having a decent website, every business owner should have a creative business card. When starting and growing a business, a professional business card is one of the essential marketing tools you may have. A business card establishes and communicates who you are and how you conduct business. A business card, among other things, is an image builder that can make a first and lasting impression on you, either positively or poorly. Many potential consumers will not take you seriously if you do not have a professional-looking business card.

Email

E-mail is a fantastic way to keep in touch with customers and increase sales. However, because most people's inboxes are complete, you'll need the correct design strategy if you want to develop your business via e-mail. Consider the e-mail's intended audience. Are you attempting to establish a business or personal relationship? Make it brief, sweet, and straightforward. Are you trying to inform your buyers about a new apparel line you've introduced? Make a few outstanding product photographs the focal point of your page.

E-newsletter/Print Newsletter

To gain a more substantial presence in the community and on the Internet, print newsletters and Internet e-newsletters (e-zines) should be written. Every business should publish a newsletter or e-zine. This will ensure that your name or brand name will frequently appear on the desktops of your most loyal customers and supporters. Everyone understands that to be successful, your potential clients must hear from you regularly; otherwise, they might forget about your brand.

Brochures

Remember to keep the potential in mind rather than your ego when developing brochures. Make sure to include a call-to-action, such as a request for an order, an appointment, information, and testimonials.

Flyers

Flyers, which can educate, promote ideas, and give a call to action, are another type of promotional material that can ensure a company's success. To make your flyers more effective, make sure the message is clear. Know and demonstrate your intentions, and support your message with a suitable typeface, headline, and graphics. Many color-coded flyers, rather than white flyers, are also quite effective and will improve your message.

Postcards

Postcard campaigns are quite effective. They're all around us on restaurant tables, automobile windshields, and grocery store bulletin boards, so take advantage of them.

Merchandizing

Other marketing materials include T-shirts, hats, bumper stickers, pens, cups, mugs, and other items that can be used to promote your brand.

Podcasting

It's only natural for businesses to incorporate podcasting into their marketing and public relations strategies. You don't have to be a high-tech firm or operator to participate. Podcasts were originally just downloadable audio blogs. Technology swiftly improved to include RSS (Really Simple Syndication), which allowed users to syndicate their content. RSS feeds are distributed over enormous networks, allowing even the tiniest businesses to have board-level visibility. Podcasting can enable your audience to listen to your message at their leisure. You'll be able to learn more about your target audience and have a better chance of them listening and paying attention when you do.

Low-cost marketing tips for your startup business

Funding is a significant challenge in most startup businesses. You are most likely to focus all the available resources on the production of your brand, making little or no funds available for marketing purposes. Here is a list of low-cost marketing techniques that can help you acquire customers:

Take advantage of free word-of-mouth promotion wherever you go. Introduce your product or services everywhere you go. Don't be shy in telling people about your product.

Compile a mailing list of everyone you meet (business cards, flyers, brochures, postcards, newsletters, etc.).

Writing articles, special reports, and columns contributes to newspapers, websites, blogs, and other publications.

Distribute press releases (also known as media and news releases).

Use print newsletters or e-newsletters/e-zines to keep your name out there (also a magazine, newspaper, etc.).

Utilize social media platforms to reach out to a larger audience.

THE POWER OF SOCIAL MEDIA IN BUSINESS MARKETING

When a startup business isn't on social media, it could miss out on valuable opportunities such as new customers, brand insights, and audience and potential relationships with customers and competitors. Furthermore, using social media to reach out to your clients in a friendly manner can be a very cost-effective strategy.

Social media emphasizes focus and the audience size and is less expensive than practically all other marketing channels. People are constantly on social media, and brands are primarily targeted based on where people are.

Facebook

Facebook is a platform with a wide range of users. A Facebook page benefits a small business owner if handled very well.

You can use Facebook to share different kinds of information, such as pictures and a company's business information. With a Facebook business page, you can leverage it to access various advertising tools and in-depth data. A lot of opportunities can be made available on a business page. You can showcase information such as your contact details, regular work hours, and the products and services you sell.

Twitter

Twitter is primarily suitable for a small number of updates, keeping in touch with followers, and sharing links to a blog post. On Twitter, information shared on this platform is ranked by videos and images. It is effortless to refer to your audience by tagging them, retweeting tweets, and liking posts.

Using a hashtag can be helpful for your information to go viral when you share it on the Twitter platform and another user with many followers retweets your content. It is advisable not to share anything irrelevant but try sharing information from other users that makes sense and is engaging.

Instagram

Instagram is a popular social media platform with a lot of users. A business may as well leverage this to showcase their business on Instagram Live or Instagram Stories. Instagram is a social media platform that focuses more on videos and photos. So, it is ideal for your business if you have a lot of visual content to showcase.

Instagram is a mobile platform.

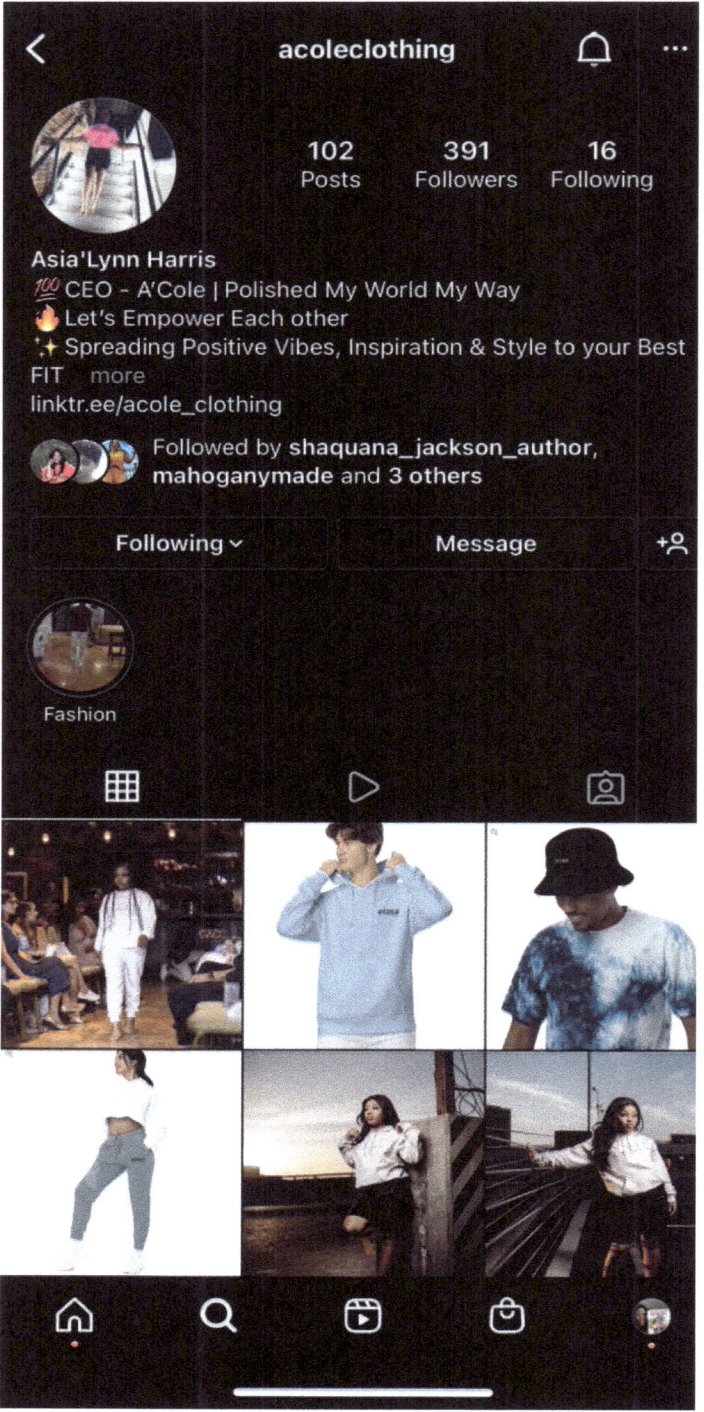

Pinterest

Rich Pins are a pin that allows marketers to add detailed information, such as product specifications and location maps to their pins. Users can save and display content by attaching digital bulletin boards arranged by category on this visually focused website. A personal user might, for example, have a food board for connecting recipes, a photography board, and so on.

Pinterest is ideal for niche businesses but not appropriate for all businesses. Craft projects, fashion, fitness, beauty, photography, and food are among the most popular categories on the website.

Snapchat

Snapchat is a phone visual social media platform that is well known for its users' content vanishing after twenty-four hours of sharing or sending pictures among friends. Messages, images, and media content are all included in the app. Snapchat material can easily be saved and uploaded elsewhere.

YouTube

This platform, now owned by Google, is primarily used for video sharing, uploading, rating, and content commenting. The site is perfect for news and entertainment.

The information on YouTube is highly educational, and producing content requires video editing software. YouTube already has engaged audiences, and businesses frequently deal with them for product placement. Because you don't have to put in the time and effort to create content and build a following, which can take years, using YouTube influencers might be a more convenient approach to selling your brand on the platform.

TikTok

TikTok is a social media platform where users create and share short videos—can be a profitable choice for businesses if used correctly. It can be challenging to achieve the correct tone to be successful as a business owner because TikTok is mainly popular with the notoriously discerning generation. If you want to create a TikTok presence, ensure you understand your brand and how it correlates to TikTok specifically. Before trying it yourself, look at how other companies use it to achieve their aim.

E-mail marketing

E-mail marketing is a simple and accessible approach to reaching your customers and offering them your items or keeping them up to date with your label's news. However, before launching an e-mail campaign, remember that sending unsolicited bulk e-mails is frowned upon, not to mention the damage that spamming will cause to your brand's image.

Permission-based e-mails are the best way to use bulk e-mailing effectively. You obtain authorization to e-mail your clients by requesting they subscribe to a newsletter.

Putting together a mailing list

The most effective way to gather e-mail addresses is to have an opt-in form on your website that invites visitors to join your mailing list. Any promotional event involving your consumers should also be used to acquire people's e-mail addresses, in my opinion. Using a standard e-mail software application to manage these e-mail addresses and send mass e-mails is tough. You'll need a mass mailing tool installed on your website's server that takes care of it.

BUILDING MY CLOTHING LINE

Let me walk you through the process of creating my clothing line and how you can use the guide on your own if you have an interest and passion for building a clothing line. First, let me brief you on how the idea of my clothing line came about.

How the Idea of A'COLE and Polished My World Came About

At the age of twelve, I became aware of the bullying that went on by other kids around me, and I wanted to spread more positivity to help students know that being different is okay, and that they are perfect just the way they are. The plan was to launch a clothing line to help spread positivity and boost self-esteem, but with my mom being a single parent, this could not be completed due to the lack of materials, equipment, and shirts we would need to start. At sixteen, the idea came back around when I realized this world needed more positivity and not just for bullying. I wanted to help others show their style with confidence, and the best way to do that is with clothing, so I relaunched because so many kids were going through depression and being uncomfortable with who they are.

Polished My World My Way represents pure positivity and confidence in your world.

With the help of my Aunt (Sade Greene), this brand was created to let others know that they can let their true personalities shine through. We also realized I am a positive person and that I could simply brand my name that would inspire others to be themselves and go after their goals, so my grandma (Iris Stagg) helped me come up with A'COLE. The meaning behind A'COLE is short and broad. Asia'Lynn is my first name, and Nicole is my middle name, so we put that together and came up with A'COLE. So, when my supporters wear this brand, they know they can be positive, just like me. When starting a business, having doubts is usually expected. You'll have doubts, especially when times get hard. When this happens, I take a step back, re-boot, and keep pushing myself to do my best.

Building my business and branding process

For the branding, we hired a Fiverr freelancer to put together the branding colors. My branding colors are black and white on my website and social media platforms. I hired a freelancer to use my slogans or brand name to have the perfect font. My mom registered my business as an LLC with the Louisiana Secretary of State and trademarked my slogan and business name. We researched wholesale clothing vendors online that have good quality so I could put my logo on them. I sell T-shirts, hoodies, joggers, crop tops, hats, and other clothing items. I also hired a freelancer to assist me in developing my social media using my brand colors. My Instagram and Facebook business pages are both well- designed—they look professional. My Instagram and Facebook handle is @Acoleclothing, and my website is www.Acolefit.com.

My mom bought a Cricut and a heat press machine to make shirts at home for customers. She also bought vinyl, which is used to print the letters on the shirts. Then she set up CashApp, PayPal, and Square, which are apps used to accept customer payments. We also met with a big box store where I want my clothing line featured. My mom also set me up with meetings with business mentors to guide us in the right direction. I also met with a big television show featuring me in the future. My mom opened accounts with some companies to get me the equipment I needed for my business, such as clothing racks, tablecloths, business cards that I used Vistaprint for, shopping bags, and a retractable size poster with my picture and business information on it.

The Building of a Website

At the very beginning of starting my brand, I created my online website through Shopify. To achieve this, I had to do a lot of research considering the fact that I, at the time, was sixteen years old and going into entrepreneurship with little experience. I had to learn to negotiate prices and partner with wholesale clothing suppliers. It was also a great experience to choose pictures of myself I wanted to display while also being able to share my story on my website.

What is Shopify?

Shopify is one of the fastest website builders to create a business website. It is easy to navigate and use, making it possible for new business owners to get a website with little effort and no coding skills required. You can consider Shopify and the advantages of their tools for quickly setting up your business website.

Benefits of Shopify:

It provides templates to assist you in creating a website faster.

It allows you to personalize templates.

Rather than employing a web designer or developer, you can save time and money by doing it yourself.

It provides a library of stock photos and videos.

It is easy to make quick changes with the help of a drag-and-drop website design tool.

It makes optimizing your website for search engines simple.

You have access to the HTML or CSS files if you want to make customization to your website.

Steps involved in starting a clothing line

The fashion industry is enormous, and you might be worried about how you will survive the competition or even the intimidation that comes with it. Don't worry! I was once at that stage, too, but the goal is to let your passion and dreams motivate you, and you will be able to succeed. You don't have to worry about your age or experience in the industry. Most of the top-notch designers we have today started with little or no experience. All you need is hard work and dedication. I will be going through the step-by-step process required to build and start your clothing line.

A business plan defines your business: It is intended to define your brand so you can understand why you started it initially. It supports you in establishing what you are about at your core and how your business relates to other businesses, allowing you to understand how you will compete.

Register your clothing line

It is important to take all the paperwork for your business seriously by doing all the necessary registration according to the state or country where you will be operating your business. Once you have done all the necessary market research, target audience, and even startup costs, you can now proceed to register your clothing line.

Product catalog

This could be one particular product or a list of products. However, it is important to consider your product list and have an effective plan for how you plan to produce, stock, and store items, and any packaging requirements.

Production equipment: Another important consideration in adequately organizing your business is production equipment. What equipment do you need to get your clothing ready? And how do you plan on getting this equipment? I will be sharing more details on the items required for clothing production later.

Create your design

Designing your clothing is one of the exciting stages in the clothing line business. If you have a design concept for a product, this is the time to start sketching it out on paper or the computer. Once you have a sketch, you can turn it into a digital sketch. This can be done using Adobe Illustrator to simplify the process for you.

Sourcing the right materials

Getting the suitable materials for your clothing line might be a bit challenging, but with proper research, you can get through it easily. You want your material to be of good quality and unique so that you can stand out among competitors.

Once you have validated the design for your clothing, you need to research your materials.

The best way to be unique in the fashion industry is to source great-quality materials. This is important for building a good reputation for your startup brand. No one will buy from a brand again if the material starts ripping or shrinking after only a few wears. To increase the chance of your customers returning to you, ensure you invest in high-quality fabrics.

You might need networking in the industry or extensive research to get a sure link to where you can get your quality materials. Remember that for your business' growth, you need to ensure you use materials that will win the hearts of your buyers.

Partner with a manufacturer

Getting the proper manufacturer to make your clothing is critical to realizing your brand's vision and growth. After all, your clothing line can't exist if you don't have a dependable manufacturer. You can have a fantastic idea, design, and cover every aspect of making your product come out perfect. However, if your manufacturer cannot meet your standards, you won't be able to maintain your quality while staying true to your concept. As a result, your brand's vision will be lost.

Consider your manufacturer's minimum order quantity, pricing, quality, and dependability when looking for a manufacturer. To streamline your procedures, look for manufacturers that have outstanding reviews. Here are some considerations before partnering with a manufacturer:

Check their reviews online.

Request samples of their fabrics.

Ask the manufacturer to show you their previous work.

Ask questions on social media and find people that have worked with them in the past.

Seek out recommendations, including businesses you can also verify on your own.

Getting the items needed for production

These are the items you will need to get your clothing ready:

Computer and phones: You will need a computer and phone to be used in the product graphics and cutting program.

Printers: This is one of the essential items you will need. Four major printers are commonly used: jet, sublimation, solvent, and laser. Solvent printers produce the best types of graphics, but they are expensive.

Graphics programs: Graphics programs such as Adobe and Canva are essential in designing custom images and artwork for your pieces. Canva is easy to navigate, and I recommend it if you plan to create your graphics.

Heat press: You will need a heat press to transfer graphics to your clothing.

Transfer paper: You will also need quality transfer paper to get images from your printer to other materials.

Cutter: A cutter and its program are needed to create stencils for screen prints. The cutter is used to cut out what you design on the cutter program.

Various methods of printing on clothing materials

There are several ways you can print designs on T-shirts, face caps, joggers, or any type of clothing you want to customize. It is crucial to know each of them before you begin your clothing line business. Understanding each type will ensure you make the right decision for your business. Below are the three major types of printing to consider for the quality production of your clothing:

Heat transfer: An image is first placed on a heat transfer paper. The paper will be cut out and then placed on the clothing material. Just like an iron that has been heated to its highest temperature, the heat transfer paper melts into the fiber of the cloth without damaging the front image. Heat transfer is a simple and quick way to get color images printed on your product.

Screen printing: This is the best option for a darker and more vibrant design. Printers are used for adding layers of ink into the material using stencils or screens, with multiple stencils for different colored inks. Due to its benefit of labor setup, screen printing is best used for large printing with many colors.

Direct to garment: Direct to garment printing involves printing ink directly onto clothing using an inkjet printer. The T-shirt design is downloaded to a computer using specialized water-based ink and transferred directly to the T-shirt with a particular printer. This is the cheapest method of printing. However, printing on each material can be time-consuming.

Therefore, this method will only be suitable for small print orders.

Pricing your products

You'll need to price your products at the end of your production stage before you can truly begin your clothing line. You'll have a better idea of how much it costs to start your clothing line once you've identified your materials and manufacturer, and you'll be able to price your items correctly.

When it comes to pricing, you will want to ensure a balance between generating a profit and setting a price that clients are prepared to pay. Your market research will influence your market; you should already know your target market, their purchasing habits, and how much they're willing to spend on your products. Remember, your pricing doesn't have to be fixed for an extended period. You can always go back and make changes.

Decide where to sell your product.

You're ready to start selling your clothing line after you've produced it and agreed on a price strategy. However, you must first determine where to sell your goods before you can begin selling them. As I mentioned earlier, you should have considered it as part of your business plan and research. Now, it's time to put it into action. As a result, if you have decided launching your business online is the best option, you will need a platform to launch and showcase your product. Consequently, selling your clothing line online will be far more cost-effective and manageable than opening a physical store. If you have success selling online, you may want to consider opening a physical storefront or marketing your brand to larger resellers, such as department shops.

You'll want to choose an e-commerce platform to establish and manage your business when you initially start online. Because the style of your online store will be vital to customers and your business, you'll want to seek platforms with unique templates. You'll also want to look for sites that can handle product variants, such as the same clothing in different sizes or colors, so you can sell your clothing line the way you want. Shopify, BigCommerce, and WooCommerce are some of the top platforms to consider in this regard.

What is a fashion show?

A fashion show is typically whatever you make it out to be. It's an environment where you not only parade different styles but it's also how you present yourself as a brand. Fashion shows are a fantastic way to showcase your clothing line and get your product to reach a larger audience.

Preparing for a fashion show can be overwhelming, especially if it is your first one. You must find good models, the proper clothing, and have adequate management during the show to make a lasting impression on the audience.

Preparing for a fashion show

My mom assists me in reaching out to the models, getting their sizes, and determining which clothing pieces we want to be displayed on the models for the fashion show. We also suggest hairstyles that would complement their outfit and practice the routine model walk with the models. I have fun because I'm also part of the show. It's my fashion show segment, starring me as well. I meet new people who not only wear my clothing line but also motivate me to keep going. I have my makeup done by a makeup artist, provided by the owner of the fashion show, along with my models. We also get our hair done by a professional who styles the models and me. We look so good, just like celebrities.

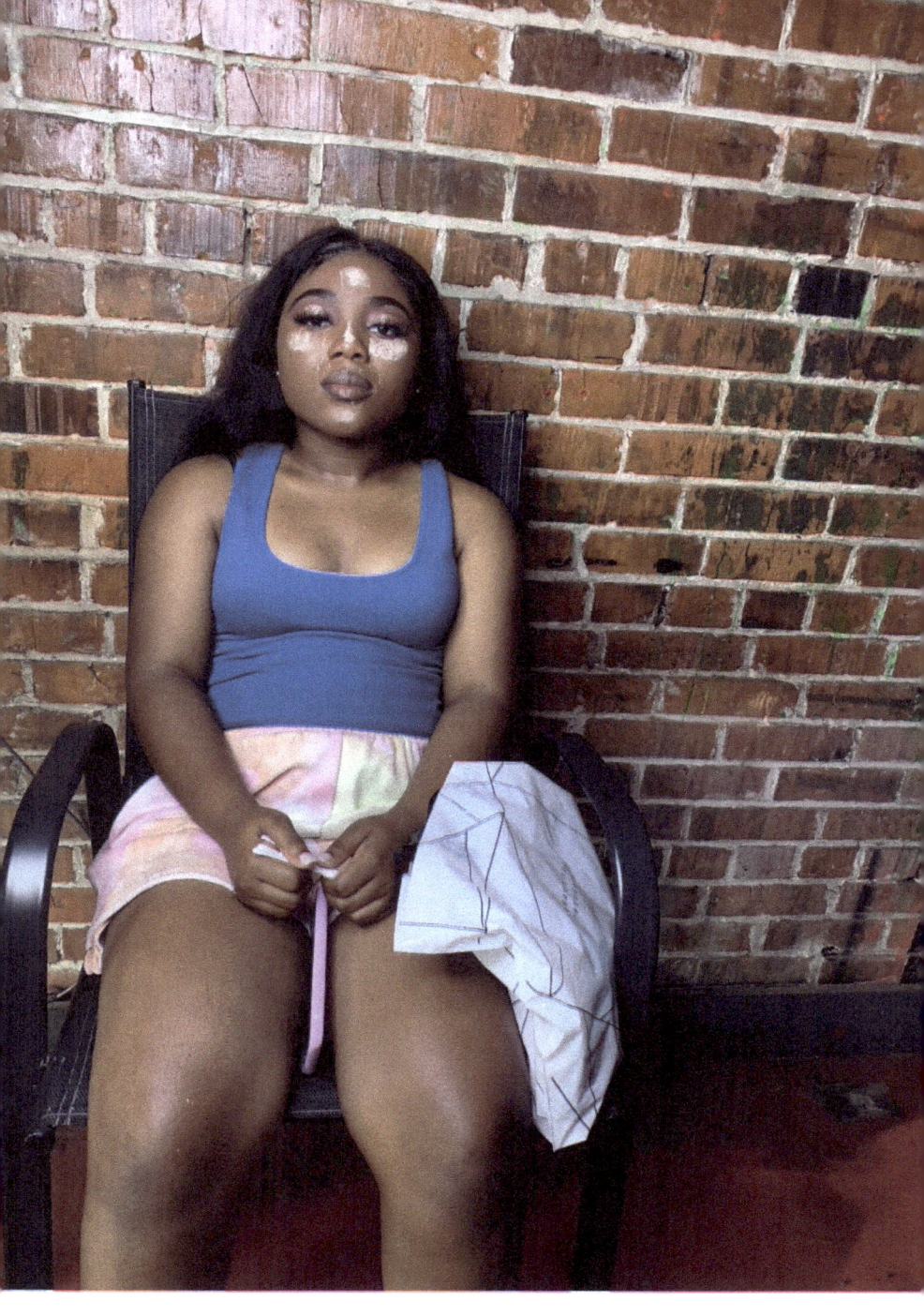

The music comes on, and we perform our model walk on stage.

Professional photographers on hand take photos of us throughout the show.

I was interviewed at the Lafayette fashion show week and had a professional video made by a company out of Atlanta.

I had extra photos of the models and me by a photographer from New Orleans. The first fashion show I modeled in and managed in my clothing section was The Aliesha Renea Fashion Show hosted in New Orleans. Since the fashion show took place during the outbreak of COVID-19, I communicated with the producer of the show and my models virtually for a while to get introduced and inquire about their sizes until it was time to meet them finally! I was able to pick out the pieces for the models who would be modeling my clothing line, A'COLE.

Tips on how to prepare for a fashion show

Choose a theme and clothing

The most important aspect of going to a fashion show is the clothing collection of your brand that you want to display. Essentially, this is the stuff you're presenting to the public, so think carefully about what you want to see on the runway from the collection.

The choice you make here will determine the success of the show. To make this easier, you can create a theme around the collection you will be showcasing. Your decision will assist you in keeping your design memorable and, of course, making sales! This can be simple if it's a seasonal show but finding a way to tie all your work together can make your presentation a huge hit.

Choosing models

Going for a fashion show is mainly to introduce your brand and reach out to more audiences. You must choose and select models that will bring your collections to life. It is crucial to remember that these models will impact the clothing line's perception in the eyes of the audience. Consider models who will stand out on the runway and leave a lasting impression on a piece of clothing.

Building a significant link between a model and a piece of clothing is a sign of success, so pursuing unique or eye-catching models is a fantastic way to add flair to your show. In addition, get started by looking for models as soon as possible! Being ahead of the game will give you a better chance of acquiring high-quality talent. Booking models may be a lengthy process at times, so being ahead of the curve will give you a better chance of securing high-quality talent. Email your models on time and communicate what you want clearly.

Create a memorable atmosphere

You want to make the fashion show a memorable opportunity for your brand. This can be done by creating a line atmosphere when your collection is displayed. Consider every element, such as music selection, models' makeup, accessories, and the general vibe, depending on the fashion show's theme.

Use your creativity and imagination! This is your opportunity to introduce your brand to the world, so, feel free to try out new ideas and develop a unique experience your target audience will love.

Socialize and network

This is the time to mingle with other designers. There is so much to learn out there. Mingle with people that will buy your product and give you recommendations and positive words to motivate you to keep going. We all need motivation, and when we get it, it encourages us to put more effort into our work. Also, enjoy the show and have fun!

Words of encouragement

You will never be able to predict what the world will bring you. You will also never know what the universe might throw your way. What you can do is prepare for the unknown and take on life's most significant missions. It is always better to grow than conform to the world's modern expectations. I believe that taking on the biggest task is equal to taking on many little ones to get to where you need to be. Cherish every step of your journey without missing a beat, and if you do, take a step back and re-boot because there is always room for improvement. Focus less on the negative, embrace the positive, and know that you are exceptional because, in the end, no one can determine your future as well as you can. Remember never to forget where you started while appreciating how far you've come. Always remain humble and faithful to yourself.

Shop A'COLE

www.Acolefit.com

www.ingramcontent.com/pod-product-compliance
Lightning Source LLC
Chambersburg PA
CBHW061207070526
44583CB00025B/3155